1994

Introduction

I feel that I have lived a life far exceeding the experiences the average person would endure. In writing these recollections of events, I am hoping to shed the pain that accompanied most, if not all experiences of my life to this point. It is my feeling that some of the best therapy that I can currently participate is sharing my experiences.

I have found that throughout each year of my life, in which I can remember details, there is something to learn. Each of these experiences has shaped the person that I have become. It has taken me more than twice as long to 'grow up' within my own eyes. I feel that once a person actually recognizes their faults and accepts that they are not mature, is when they have actually matured enough in life to be a respectable adult.

Throughout my life there have been more challenges than I wish upon any person, and most are from my own actions. I blame no one but myself for a majority of my experiences once I reached the age of legal adulthood and was thrust onto the streets ill-equipped to survive.

I hope to finish each book as a year within my own life, detailing what experiences that I can still remember in detail. I will warn you now, there are many.

Foreword

One of the most eventful years of my life, of which I almost did not survive. With serious threats upon my life, many poor decisions, all which were completely avoidable. But I was incapable of understanding any of the consequences of my actions or decisions.

In 1994, I was exposed to dangerous gangs, guns, drugs, and two near death experiences. I was nearly executed twice in one night. I experienced political activities within my county's legal system and pressure from the police. I survived it all, but still carry the weight of it all to this day. These memories are still present and fear is triggered by daily activities.

This year had to come first, since it also includes the first step of the rest of my life. I'm not about to tell you that life was all peaches and cream from the end of this book. Instead I will tell you that I started to see the right path, even though it took me much longer to follow that path.

Contents

I was just released from jail, again

This wasn't my first time, and turns out that it wouldn't be my last. This time was slightly different though, as I had a plan to get my life in order. While in jail I had time to reflect on the previous few months that had put me into that position. Not to mention I had a little bit of money coming my way due to a small financial settlement, I should have enough money in about a week to start my life over. But that week was the big question mark.

My mother said she would try to get there to give me a ride, but again was delayed due to my step-father Jim. She was telling him that she had to run to the store for milk, but it was taking longer to get out of the house after preparing him dinner. So I started walking, in the snow toward the direction she would be coming.

I was arrested during the late summer in Alabama, extradited to Illinois, and it was now winter; it was COLD. I had a light t-shirt and sweatpants, the same attire that I was wearing when I was arrested, and still wearing when I got out of the inmate transportation van. One of the guards that I befriended (lost card games to), gave me one of the old heavier jail shirt tops to get me out of the lobby.

My release was in the evening, after 5pm, there was no sun and a cold snowy wind was at my face as I walked. I nearly got to the interstate about a mile down from the jail when I spotted her car. She turned around and picked me up and we went to the store for milk, as I'm sure my step-father would notice had she not. This is when I was told that she decided to not discuss me with my step-father Jim and that I would have to stay elsewhere. I had looked forward to staying at 'home' during this week to hopefully get advice on my new start. This would not be the case.

While walking through the store, she called her cousin to ask a favor and allow me to stay with her for a short time.

Sue was a strong woman who demanded respect, which I would always give to this day. She raised her children in a part of town which I would never dream of travelling today. Her kids were raised with manners and the fear of god which she drove into them.

I was always apprehensive when staying at her house, which I had done a couple times at a much younger age. I had no other option, so I accepted graciously.

When my mother dropped me off at Sue's house, this is the first I had seen her in quite a few years. She had moved to a much better area in town and wasn't too far from a familiar area to me. I was reintroduced to her son Christopher who she called downstairs from his room.

I hadn't seen Christopher in years

Christopher seemed to be a strong guy, younger than me, and showed respect right from the start. The last time I saw Christopher, I hadn't really interacted with him. I would estimate his age at eight to nine years old the last we saw each other, now eighteen or nineteen, and I had memories of his level of activity back then; full of energy. With no expectations, I went upstairs with him to his room.

I found that the whole upstairs consisted of two adjoining rooms directly at the top of the stairs. Both rooms upstairs were his and the first room was a larger of the two. Typical teen bedroom for the time, containing things like a bed, posters, a stereo system blasting music, and a weight bench. The second room would be mine to use for the time, containing a nightstand by the window and a bunk bed, nothing more -- a place to crash.

Also in the bedroom when I arrived were three other guys, all approximately the same ages between 18-19 years old. Once the door closed, the music went up and the chorus started singing along with the stereo. I plopped down on the edge of the bed as Christopher introduced me as his cousin. During the introductions, a joint appeared and started to be passed around.

Contrary to popular belief, not everyone my age at the time smokes pot all the time. When I passed without taking a hit, I received a few odd looks from the other guys, but that was soon dismissed as I replied "Jesus, I just got out of jail and haven't even figured out where I'm sleeping yet".

I lit a cigarette from the pack of smokes my mother bought me before dropping me off. I did however drink a forty that was offered, and sat smoking cigs and listening to rap music all night. "Insane in the membrane, insane in the brain" still rings through my head to this day as I recollect those days. Impossible to forget considering where it all leads.

The next morning my mother came through again. She had a bag of my clothes, and to this day I do not know how she got them. She brought it to the house and left shortly after getting in the door. She also brought me another pack of smokes. I figure it was one of her frequent cigarette or milk runs again. Later in the day I called my lawyer who handled my settlement to arrange an appointment to pick up my check. It would have to wait a few days as he was unavailable.

All hell broke loose

The following night is when everything went to hell. As usual, we were up in Christopher's bedroom listening to music and doing a whole lot of nothing. At some point, one of the guys said that they needed to walk to the store to get more cigarettes. As they got up, I realized that meant we were all going. So I headed down the stairs and out the door with them.

We walked past several neighborhood taverns which were open and had sold cigarettes over the counter or vending machines. The goal was to get out of the house and get fresh air, was my assumption. I still do not know to this day why we walked in the cold winter air at such a late hour, but we finally reached the gas station many blocks from where we started. Only to turn around and start heading back towards the house, but on a different path.

We walked south down Broadway St, which was a fairly large four lane state highway. The road was populated with houses, small businesses and car repair shops on one side. The other side used to have nearly the same, but was very close to a steep bluff overlooking the I&M Ship Canal. The occasional house still stood along the road, but most had been long gone.

As we neared the area to turn west and return to the house, we were near a few car repair shops with small parking areas out front. Due to the hour, there had not been much traffic on the road. To me, the area was foreign as I had never been in the area this late or on foot. There was a vehicle coming northbound in the far lane that started to slow as it approached. One of the guys walking with us started to wave at the small SUV and yelled something, but I didn't really hear it or see the wave. Only a brief movement out of the corner of my eye as I looked toward the next block for our upcoming turn.

I heard the engine rev and the SUV turned into the parking lot across the road and the passenger was yelling something back. The next thing I heard scared the shit out of me, literally. I left a rosebud in my shorts the moment I heard the first shot ring out. Dropping to my knees, crawling behind a car parked at the lot we were passing, I saw one of the guys that I was walking with running with a small machine gun that I would later learn was a mac-11 submachine gun. I had only heard of a mac-10 from the TV. I had never heard gunfire like that before that wasn't at an outdoor gun range when I was younger, or on television. It was chilling, and as I said before, rosebud. I was later told that the people in the vehicle shot first, but in my mind it did not matter. I was scared. The SUV took off as if the driver had just put his foot through the floorboard. The guy hiding beside me yelled that there was a fence behind us, so we took off over the fence and ran through dark alleys and people's back yards. I don't recall exactly where we were when it all happened, and surely don't remember how we got back to the house.

The moment we got back, we all went immediately upstairs into Christopher's bedroom. There was nobody else in the rest of the house. I was basically left out of the following conversation as the other guys were talking slightly under what I could hear on the other side of the room over the music that was still playing. I had assumed that both shooters were terrible shots and completely missed their targets. None of the guys I was with got hit, and after finally accepting the joint I was offered, I passed out on the bottom bunk in the room I was occupying. Even with the assistance of weed and beer, I still didn't fall asleep for a long time. This still haunts me to this day.

My next sight that night was a flashlight in my eyes, with a police officer standing over me. He did not have his gun drawn, but was poking me with what I assume was a baton. I recognized my situation immediately and didn't move after my eyes finally focused and I woke up, instantly sober. Being handcuffed and led out of the house, I knew that somebody in that SUV didn't get away unharmed.

Locked inside a tiny room again

After many hours of interrogation, I was released. I found out while being questioned, that the shooter gave the mac-11 to another friend who wasn't there that night. Christopher called him to come get the gun and hide it. Even though Christopher was not the shooter, his involvement with hiding the weapon was enough to get him charged with some serious offenses. I learned during questioning that the friend that was going to hide the weapon, was stopped on the street while travelling back to his house carrying the gun. He was quick to tell the story of the events and named names the moment the police asked. He didn't know my name, so I assume that helped keep me out of what came next.

My name was never in the story, except when the police asked about me. They knew I was there, but it was obvious that I had no clue what was happening and had no idea the gun was even present. I still to this day believe that all of those guys told the truth and kept me out of their mess. Even the police must have figured that my past, that I just got out of jail, and my involvement was so minimal that there was no way I was involved. I was honestly shocked that I walked out of that police station without something following me, especially knowing how the legal system works in that city and county.

That doesn't mean that when I got home I didn't have to answer questions. I was questioned by Sue as well as the family of the actual shooter about what happened. But I couldn't answer for things I did not know. Even after the event that night, I cleaned my shorts and smoked a joint so I could sleep, hoping nothing came of it.

Later that same night, two guys Rudy and Casey came over. They were inseparable and typically part of Christopher's group of friends. They weren't there that night, but came to talk to me. They had questions and as we talked, we got to know each other. It wasn't long after that, I started staying with Rudy and his father when I felt my welcome was wearing out with Sue, whose son was now in jail pending attempted murder charges. She had also mentioned that she was going to move soon and I would have to figure out where to stay. I occasionally stayed there anyway, so I wouldn't completely wear out my couch spot at Rudy's house. But the house was empty except for me, for the most part. In the meantime, my check finally came in and I was trying to figure out how to make it work. It wasn't the amount I was told, so my original plan wasn't going to work. But I knew that no matter what, a car had to come first.

Two cars in one month

Transportation in this area is a requirement, so I purchased a used late 1989 Ford Thunderbird with most of the settlement money. It was what I could afford and still hopefully have enough money to do something.

That car lasted almost a week before it was fire-bombed in front of Sue's house. I slightly woke to a noise outside. Your brain processes things you hear that are out of the ordinary, and glass shattering along with crackles and pops, tends to wake you up. Not that I slept very soundly at this point anyway, but I recall a slow realization and seeing that  is my car burning at the curb. I still think that it was retaliation for the victim of the shooting. He was hit from a shot through the firewall of that little SUV and was still in the hospital. I do not know what ever happened to him or who he was, only that he survived. If he would have died, the charges against Christopher and the shooter would have been much worse.

I had insurance on the car, but it wasn't enough. At my age, the insurance premium was much higher than I could afford. But with the settlement check, I was trying to think like a responsible adult.   But the insurance company suspected fraud and extremely limited the coverage and paid out extremely little. I lost any hopes of starting over, having to return to the dealership to buy a  back-lot Mazda B2200 with severe body damage. This was back in the day when all dealers had what they called a "wholesale lot" for people like me. Meaning you could buy the scraps that people dragged off the streets during their "push it, pull it - we take anything on trade" promotions. I spent my last few dollars buying that, so I could have something to sleep in.

That's when I met Ishmael

I had already been on the hunt for work, but my living situation was making it very difficult to do. I had since made contact with a previous neighbor whom I was able to arrange to buy pot on credit to get me started earning some cash. We had a few years of trust built from when we were neighbors. I had made a few trips back and forth with him, buying and selling until I didn't need the credit anymore. I continued to sell the product so I could eat more than leftovers or whatever someone gave me.

Over the following weeks, I was introduced to Ishmael. An older guy who we started to run into at parties, where I was often invited due to my 'party favors'. At one of these parties, I found myself in the back seat of Ishmael's car driving around town chatting. The subjects ranged from people I knew and did not know, to my history and abilities. He seemed to be a trustworthy person and I felt comfortable. I let my guard down and basically gave him a detailed list of my life experiences to that point, which by them amount to 'not much'. But something I had said piqued his interest.

I briefly recall a night when the two of us travelled to a far north suburb to bail out his friend from jail. No mention of the charges or anything of the sort. But the long ride in the car, chatting as we went, I felt we got to know each other. On the way back, the three of us stopped at Taco Bell and hammered down a tray full of tacos. I remember a dare or bet on who could eat the most tacos, which I won easily. I was always hungry.

One night he picked me up for what I assumed was a party or just a cruise around town sipping on forties. But no, he wanted me to meet someone that he knew. We met outside the Sams' Club in a big dark area of the parking lot. I wasn't nervous at all, since we typically sat in dark parking lots or alleys to not be disturbed by the law. A large brand new pickup truck pulled up alongside his car, and as you can visualize was much taller than allowed for a quiet car-to-car discussion. We got out and hopped into his large truck.

I was sitting in the passenger seat next to the 'guy'. I do not recall his name, but remember his wavy red hair and unkempt curly haired patchy beard. Ishmael was sitting directly behind me from which I heard, "this is the guy".
He says, "So you are THE GUY". Immediately I start reaching into my hoodie pocket and feeling around for a nickel bag of weed that I always had at the ready. But before my

hand comes out of my pocket, he blurts out "I hear you are good with computers?". That was unexpected.

In my past, I was exposed to computers and had for a while engulfed myself with nearly everything I could in order to learn more. But due to my recent life experiences, it is sad to say that none of it was for the greater good. I had put my knowledge together with what I had experienced in the criminal world. I had grand ideas on how to defraud and steal, but just hadn't gotten around to it yet. This was my chance, even though I was not completely ready for it. He had accumulated a massive debt on a credit card while remodeling his house. This was his problem, and strangely enough I had given Ishmael my ideas over the course of our discussions.

The plan was simple enough, but somewhat tricky to implement. I had thought that I knew enough and could get it done. So we made a plan and I had some requirements, which was met with little to no resistance. That night we visited the local OfficeMax, which was the only place nearby to buy a decent computer at the time. That night I was checked into a motel paid for by Ishmael. The plan was to make a huge chunk of his credit card debt disappear, which I was confident would work.

Over the course of two weeks I had worked out everything that I needed, except one detail. It was that detail that completely prevented this idea from working. I was actually scared at this point since I knew that I owed for the computer as well, the living arrangements and food that was provided. I had sometimes let that fear escape my mind and Ishmael was without a doubt aware. He started hanging around more and more as I made calls, investigated my planned target's weakness, and worked out the details on the computer.

Even today I will not go into detail on how I thought it would work, but the idea from my standpoint seemed flawless. My single flaw was the only thing standing in the way, and was the size of a mountain. But the overall idea was to force refunds using the primary store's payment system, which for obvious reasons I could not gain access.

I was still selling weed throughout this time, as it seemed like that market was increasing. I spent less time at the motel and more visiting parties delivering my product in the beat up Mazda pickup truck. More than a few times, Ishmael was at these parties as well as a few more faces I saw repeatedly. I was the "weed guy" and Bo was the "coke guy". The area was in drought conditions and we were it… at the time.

Eventually, cocaine became more readily available but weed was still scarce. Luckily my source was outside of this circle and I started to build up some funds. I was looking to clear myself from Ishmael and his friend, paying for my expenses that I incurred. But there just wasn't enough time.

When you owe, you pay the price

Ishmael came to my motel room one night and told me that his brother needed to talk to me. I had a blink of fear, which he identified and assured me that it had nothing to do with my current failure. But he knew it was a failure, so that kept me apprehensive about this meeting. I KNEW his brother by name and reputation, we had been at quite a few of the same parties. In today's terms, you would call him the 'shot caller' for the Vice Lords street gang in our area. He was very well known, just not by me other than by name.

When I stepped outside the motel room and walked to Ishmael's car, there was somebody already in the passenger seat. Mauricio was sitting there waiting. If he had been sitting in the back seat or anyone else in the car, I would have bolted for the tree line across the parking lot. But he was in the passenger seat of an empty car, and motioned for me to sit behind him. That put me somewhat at ease.

We drove for about twenty minutes before the idle chatter turned to the point of the meeting. Mauricio knew that I "owed", and he also knew that I had a customer base for my weed sales that they couldn't reach. Being a fairly clean and innocent looking white guy, I was what he needed, and he assumed was my primary customer base. They had acquired a substantial amount of cocaine that they needed to sell quickly. The reason was to bail out one of their higher up gang members before his trial so he could skip bail and run to Mexico. I was shocked that I was let in on that information, and strangely I felt honored that they trusted me like that. I was young and did not understand the whole situation, how wrong that feeling was. Then came the pressure.

I told him that at best I might be able to sell an ounce in a week, maybe. Nothing near the amount they needed me to sell. I sold to guys my age that I knew in passing at the pool hall or previously worked with, or at the same parties that they attended. Nowhere near the clientele they needed me for, far from it. They had an image in their mind that would be able to access the rich white party kids from the 'good' side of town. This was never the case. But there were threats, serious ones, that involved family members. I was extremely protective of those I considered family, even though they never really felt the same towards me. Mauricio and Ishmael knew of them all, even the ones I never mentioned. But I know how information gets around and they had it, so there was no hiding. I had to do it, and agreed.

Within minutes we arrived back at the motel. As I exited the back seat and walked toward the front of the car, the passenger window lowered and Mauricio called my name. "Where are you going?", and he waved me to come back to the car. In his lap was what looked like a plastic grocery bag, which he handed me and told me "I expect my money in the morning", and he closed the window as Ishmael backed out and they drove away.

I peeked into the bag and caught a glimpse of small white baggies, packed tight with white powder. I was standing in the motel parking lot, not exactly the place to be looking at this sort of thing. Once I caught that glimpse, I shoved the grocery bag into my coat and headed straight for the room. Once inside, I removed the contents. Twelve sandwich baggies, cocaine tightly packed into the corner of each bag closed with a tight knot.

I was freaking out, what the hell could I do with that!? And by morning? I did the first thing anyone would do, I called a friend. Or at least who I thought was a friend, for advice.

Rudy and Casey showed up, immediately wanting to party the moment they heard the story. Totally disregarding my situation, and now them by association. After telling them to get lost, I had to think of another plan. They told me that they were going over to a different motel where their girlfriends had gotten a room to have a small 'motel party', which was common for the time.

I called my weed supplier. Thankfully he did buy some of the product, but nowhere near what I needed to make disappear. But now I had over four thousand dollars in my pocket, hopefully that would help when the morning came and the remainder was still unsold.

When I got back to the motel, I was greeted by the motel manager at the door telling me that the week's rate had not been paid. After covering that out of the four thousand, I noticed Ishmael's car outside. He was there to check on me and to remind me "ALL OF IT". I had nowhere to go, so I joined Rudy and Casey at the other motel. I became the discussion of the night at their little party.

One of the girls suggested that I reach out and contact Bo. He sold all the time and maybe he could take some off my hands, even if it is for a lesser amount than could be obtained on the street. I had no choice, so without hesitation she made the call.

Within an hour Bo showed up outside the motel room and I stepped outside to talk. As soon as he heard of the quantity, he backed away shaking his head saying "boy, you in deep now. But I got you". He said that his brother or cousin near "The City", who could take that weight and he would put in the call for me. I felt relieved thinking that soon I would be out and I could drop the cash from the proceeds and disappear quickly before they tried to get me to do it again.

My relief was short lived and I almost paid with my life at that motel. When arrangements were made, I suggested another motel room but within the same motel. Knowing that you can pay a bit extra cash for a room without ID, I went to the desk and got a room right around the corner. I grabbed a small box that was in my truck and dumped my pockets, putting the box under the bed of the room I just rented before returning to the party room. All I had to do was wait for the call, as his guy was on the way and the trip should take about an hour. Bo had left already, but said that he would be there for the meet.

This wouldn't be my first time tonight

When the phone rang, I nearly jumped out of my skin as the others got a giggle from it. I walked out of the room and around the side of the building toward the meeting room. I spotted Bo's car sitting right beside another car and the two were talking. I opened the door and motioned them inside. The discussion was quick and to the point. He asked how much I had and what I wanted for it. When I told him the quantity and price, he agreed and told me to grab it. Waiting for him to approach the door to go get the money, I noticed that he wasn't moving. There was no way that he was carrying that amount of cash on him. I also noticed that Bo stepped back as if to get out of the way of something. That's when I spotted the pistol in this guy's hand pointing at me.

He cold cocked me with the butt of the pistol. I spun around from the blow and went down on my face like a tree crashing to the ground during a storm. After a moment I came around to him tapping me on the back of the head with the barrel of the pistol. Without delay, I slowly pointed under the bed, where I could see the box clearly from my position. He instructed me to get it, which I did without hesitation but slowly. As the box emerged from under the bed, I felt a crushing weight on my body as he dropped his knee into the small of my back.

My face was toward the nightstand beside the bed, so I could not see a thing, only a shadow from the overhead light above the small table by the window. I saw it coming, the shadow of a gripped pistol swinging to the back of my head. This was the first time in my life I have been knocked unconscious, but unfortunately not the last.

I awoke to a splitting headache, blood soaked face from the first hit, and a massive lump on the back of my head from the second. I was alone in the room with the lights on and the door standing wide open. An empty box lying beside me on the floor, no cash in my pocket, but my truck keys and wallet were still in my pockets. But no sign of Bo, as I expected. As I exited the room, I noticed that there were no cars in the parking lot either, not surprising, I already knew what had happened. I got rolled for four thousand bucks and eight ounces of powder.

When I returned to the other 'party' room, the girls helped me clean up my wounds and the guys told me that I need to let Mauricio know right away. Rudy assured me that 'shit happens' and they'll have my back. They know Bo better than I do, will know where to find him, and will handle it. He assured me that I'll be fine, to just make contact. So I make the call, partially explain the situation without details over the phone, which I am told to meet at the original motel and they would pick me up and they'll handle it. I left reassured that everything would be alright and that I am a friend to them.

I made the worst call of my life, so far

I had gone directly to the motel to meet them and they arrived before I had a chance to get inside. But they came into the room anyway and started looking around. Loudly noting that there were no signs of struggle and no blood. I clarified that it was the other motel and told them the story again with details since we weren't on a phone. There was shock on Mauricio's face and a grumble that I barely heard, but I recognized him repeating the name 'Bo' preceded by profanities in Spanish.

Within minutes, we were all in an older full size sedan in near perfect condition, which is common and not only portrayed in movies. There was another car full of guys following, but they waited outside of the room and never got out. In the back seat, they are discussing something just out of my hearing range, just under the music. We made a quick stop at the other motel so they could see the 'meet room', where they saw the blood. After leaving, we slowly cruised across town which took a little while as I was staying on the west side of town, they were all from the east side of town.

They said that they know exactly where Bo is and they are familiar with his people. They were going to pay them both a visit and resolve this. Since it was my mess, I would have to be there and I would have to get payback for my injuries, that was the way it was going to happen. We drove into a dark lot behind a house that I had seen from the road in passing. I drove this route to my own supplier, so I was somewhat familiar with the area. I had never paid much attention to this house, but it wasn't the house we were visiting. There was an old carriage house out back that still functioned as a shed. I was told that they were stopping to pick up guns for protection during the planned encounter. One of the guys jumped out of a second car and tried to open the door, which was chained closed. He still peeked inside and said that it's packed with too much junk and there's no way we'd get inside.

We got back on the road and there was further discussion. For a third time, the cellular bag phone that one of the guys was carrying started to ring. He immediately passed the handset to Mauricio, who relayed to the other guys that they had found Bo and were keeping an eye on him. Mauricio replied that we were on the way.

It was a small house with a double wide driveway along the side with space for at least six cars. The color of the house was nearly impossible to make out, but I wouldn't doubt white or beige vinyl siding due to the commonality of that color in the area. We parked near the side of the house and there was a door right beside the car, but we walked to the front door anyway. Nothing strange, and I was told again that we were picking up guns for our trip and that I should come inside to help. I followed without question, out of fear or stupidity, take your pick.

We crossed the tiny living room, past the small attached kitchen heading down the hallway. There was a light on inside the first bedroom, but we were passing that, heading toward the dark back room. The guy in front of me walked right past the room. Across from that room was a bathroom. I caught a glimpse from the corner of my eye of something coming at me, beyond the blurry vision from the previous knocks to my head. I knew what had just happened, as I was knocked into the bedroom and tripped over Bo who was laying on the floor beaten and bloody. When I tripped I fell on the tiny twin size bed within the room.

I surely wasn't going to survive

I longed for the interrogation the police had subjected me to a little while back. This was something totally different. Every question was preceded with a hit to the face, a pistol in my mouth, or a heavy iron weight to the head. Following the question was more of the same, and also came after an answer was given. No matter what was said, no matter if they believed you, you still received the same. I was duct taped at the wrists to prevent me from blocking the blows to my face or head. My ankles were taped together to prevent me from kicking to the side. Eventually I was taped around the head with a sock in my mouth to shut me up. I was definitely crying and moaning in pain, which gained more attention and more blows. They eventually stopped working me over and moved on. Bo had received the same, but in my recollection I think that they believed me as his beatings were getting worse. They somewhat stopped questioning me and went to work on him. This lasted for hours, Bo's lasted about twenty minutes longer than my beatings, but it seemed like days. Then suddenly, it stopped.

We were told that we did good and we could be trusted. They were taking us to the hospital and would drop us out in front of the emergency room, and to not say a word or they would start again where they just finished.

I was led out of the room directly behind Bo, who was being carried by two guys. I was being carried too, but made more of an effort to stand and walk. Even though I was still taped, my big feet allowed for somewhat of a shuffle. Being carried sideways under my arms and down the hall, we moved through the house. We went out through the side door of the house this time, but passed by the last car in the driveway. As soon as we passed the passenger door, even though the blood pouring into my eyes blocked my vision, I could see that the trunk of the car was open and Bo was being pushed inside. When I saw that, I jerked back into the arms of the guy who had pushed me through the house. He told me to shut up and get in, they didn't want blood inside the car and that we would be pulled out at the hospital. But I knew better, as I've probably seen the same movies they got this whole idea from.

As the car drove, the tail lights cast a red glow all throughout the trunk. Being an older car, there was plenty of space. Beyond the blood I could see Bo, and he wasn't moving. I knew he was still alive since he was whimpering and moaning, undoubtedly in severe pain, with the same sock and duct tape job. I realized that the blood from my face had soaked my wrists and arms enough to loosen the grip of the duct tape. I was able to get my arms free. Since the driver of the car was preoccupied with driving and the music was incredibly loud to cover any noise we might make, I was able to get myself and Bo completely free of our bonds.

I put my face to his ear and asked if he could hear me, which he nodded yes. We had to get out of this trunk, but it wasn't going to happen while the car was moving. This car was from a day without safety features other than seatbelts, so an interior trunk release was not a thing. Besides that, I doubt I would have considered it at this point. I told Bo that I would be springing from the trunk and running the first moment I could. Run with everything you have, don't stop. Even though I knew that Bo was the cause, something in the back of my brain still registered him as a human being.

Right before the car came to a stop, I noticed that the music stopped. I could hear two guys in the front talking. "Yeah, this should work". And the trunk lit up with white light from the car's reverse lights. They were backing in somewhere, and there was no emergency room that they would be backing into. That solidified my suspicion and I knew we had to fight or die.

The trunk opened and a pair of hands reached in quickly, before any chance to react. The hands got ahold of Bo's shirt and yanked him from the trunk. That's when I saw the revolver for the first time, just as you see in the movies. Shining silver, lit by the street light not far off, a long beefy barrel, pointed directly at my face. Either they knew we unbound ourselves, didn't realize it happened, or just didn't care. I was told to get out of the trunk. As I threw a leg over, Bo sprang into action and struggled with the first guy, who was not holding a gun.

His face still haunts me today

This is the first time I had seen Roman. He was shorter than either of his brothers Mauricio or Ishmael. Short and fairly skinny, with black hair that was out of control for the most part. If I were to describe his look, it would be bat-shit crazy. And in the situation now, I would not be wrong. As he stood between myself and any escape with a large pistol in his hand being raised towards  me, but at the same time his head was beginning to turn towards the struggle between the other guy and Bo. Everything was moving in slow motion right now, at least in my memory. I'm sure it was moving real-time when it all happened.

As Roman turned to help subdue or shoot Bo, I sprung the rest of the way out of the trunk and rushed Roman, knocking him into Bo and the other guy. My next destination was visible, I recognized it, and I went for it as fast as I could.

I am by no means afraid of water, especially under these circumstances. It did not matter that it is called a 'sanitary canal' for obvious reasons, that it is the dead of winter, or that I was wearing heavy winter clothes. None of that registered and I went for it. As soon as I was knee deep in the water, I dove head first away from the gunfire that now erupted behind me. I heard another shot while I was underwater. But as with frigid cold water, the shock to my system was too much and I came up gasping for air as my lungs contracted. Pulling myself farther away from shore with my arms and kicking as hard as I could, I could hear more shots. But I was getting away, come hell or high water, literally. I turned back to face their direction when the shots stopped, to see them get into the car and speed away. I could see Bo laying in the road by the riverbank.

As I got out of the water, I approached Bo who was still alive. The same moaning and whimpering in pain, added by crying and screaming at this time. I looked around and there was no place to go. One house, row-style house built atop it's cellar with a very tall stairway leading to the porch and front door. This isn't the neighborhood to expect assistance, and definitely not one you pound on doors in the wee hours of the morning. But I did what I had to do, and hobbled up the stairs.

I banged on that door screaming for help, but nobody answered and I don't blame them. But I must assume that they called the police. After the stairway ascent, banging on the door with my fists, and my descent back to street level to search other sources of help, a police siren could be heard in the distance. I made my way to the center of the road just as the squad car arrived with lights and sirens lighting up the whole street. The car slid to a stop on the snow and ice covered road. I dropped to my knees and fell forward on my face in exhaustion. The cold car-tire compacted snow on the street felt warmer than the rest of my river soaked body. I yelled to the officer that there was another man farther down behind me. The second squad car came from the other direction and found Bo.

We both had been beaten, pistol whipped, and shot at. Bo took three bullets to his abdomen, and I was grazed on my right leg, and hit by another water cushioned shot to the shoulder. I never saw Bo again after this night, but I heard his name a few times in passing and had heard he still lived in the area.

I was taken to the hospital, interrogated again, and shuffled over to the prosecutor's office. I was met by two gentlemen that identified themselves as the State's Attorney and an Assistant State's Attorney, who said they were part of the county gang task force. Before they could complete their question, I had already answered "Yes, I will testify". Having been born and raised in this county, I knew the pressure they could put on me. As well as knowing other attempts would be made on my life if I were to refuse to talk and subsequently go to jail.

Am I a victim or a defendant?

I was considered a material witness, as well as a victim. But the police claimed to have found several baggies of cocaine in the motel room where I was sleeping. But I can guarantee that it did not exist. Everything I had was stolen, spurring this whole ordeal. The gang members who were in the room the night before surely would have found it too. But this gave the State's Attorney's office plenty of ammunition, would it be needed for pressure, should I not comply.

We discussed all details from the previous night and into the morning, as well as discussing what precautions I would need to take to ensure my survival. The general consensus was that I would leave town and return when called for the trial(s). It was understood that I could not financially afford to go anywhere, but they were also in contact with my mother, from information I provided at the hospital earlier. There was no way that I would be allowed, or should I stay, with her. But she had convinced them that she was fully capable of protecting me.

I was finally dumped into a local fleabag motel that nearly everyone I know has forgotten about.

I can't remember who got me a room or paid for it, but I walked in and dropped onto the bed. When I woke up I thought it was the same day, but I had slept through the night and into the next afternoon. But I still don't remember any of it.

I cannot begin to describe the pain I was experiencing. The hospital had given me a couple of pain pills, but not nearly enough. When I woke up, I felt every impact that my broken body had received. From the stitches across the bumps on my head, a mouth full of cracked teeth, and down to the frostbite on my toes. Everything hurt, but there wasn't anything that I could do about it. My state of shock when I was in the emergency room probably caused me to tell them that it didn't hurt very much. But that was a lie.

I don't recall how it all happened after that, but I remember making some phone calls and arranging a few days at a friend's house that I hadn't spoken to for a long while. His family had agreed to take me in for a few days until I could figure something out, but that translated to a single overnight. I somehow got over to his house and my mother was involved in retrieving my old Mazda pickup truck from the motel. I do recall slipping into the parking lot and a city police car was parked in the lot. Then came the long indirect drive back to the friend's house.

Later that evening, we visited an auto parts store to buy several cans of flat black spray paint. Giving the old junk Mazda a low class camouflage flat black makeover. It went from the original factory light blue with sporty stripes, to a flat black rattle can 'lipstick on a pig' color. With paint running from every corner and edge, it finally dried by the next morning in time for me to head out.

A plan was hatched to take a cruise for a few hours pointed southeast towards my aunt's house, my mother's sister. My mother told me that she was going to let me hide out there for a while to get a job and on my feet. It's not like I had anything to pack since all of my belongings were already in the truck except for the backpack that held my overnight stuff. Within an hour of that news, I was on the road.

Just springtime in Indiana

There was no great reunion in seeing my aunt again, as I hadn't seen her in a very long time. She had made trips up to see my mother, and my mother and her family had gone down for small partial family reunions. But I was never invited to those, another one of those 'step-father side effects'.

When I got into town, it was late afternoon and I had to locate the Eagles Lodge. In a small town like this it shouldn't be too difficult, but the fact that the popular entrance to the building was actually a small parking lot accessed from the alley, made it difficult. My Aunt managed the bar situated inside the lodge and was still on her dayshift bartending. I sat at the bar and just a brief hug across the bar was all I got, which didn't seem right. Whenever we did get together, there had always been a solid hug that lasted a lot longer than this one did. That right there, gave me pause and I knew something was coming.

This is when she told me that it was never agreed that she would take me in. Her husband at the time had overheard the conversation and nixed that thought before my mother got off the phone. All she had said is that if I were down there, she would keep an eye on me. But it was her understanding that I would be able to care for myself. Another one of those "spoiled kid" misconception events that spanned my whole life, leaving me on the sidelines again.

She stayed a little while after work to chat about what had happened. Even though I had no plans or resources, she left me sitting at the bar with a coke she had bought me. I sat for about an hour with no idea what I would possibly do. I finally called my mother to relay the information about my aunt and that I would find a place to park the truck for the night. This is when she agreed to pay for a motel for me, so I could figure something out.

I spent one week in that motel, and got signed on with a temporary agency two days later. My days were spent at the Lodge with my aunt, and my evenings were spent working. My position at the factory involved self-inflicted cuts on my fingers (from aluminum radiator fins) received while installing molded overflow bottles on new radiators. The company made radiator assemblies for brand new Chrysler vehicles. It was a temporary job, so the pay was terrible. On top of that, I would run out of food and housing well before the first paycheck came.

I only slept in the truck once this winter

The day after I slept in the truck, I received an offer from Linda. She was a small woman who lived in the house directly behind the Lodge, and spent her days drinking White Russians. She was receiving disability payments to live and support her high school aged daughter. I still have no idea what her disability was, but I saw no signs of any limitations. Linda has been at the bar every day that I was there, and had overheard all of my discussions with my aunt. Even though we only had small idle chats that you would expect at a neighborhood bar, she felt that she knew enough and that she could help.

She offered to let me stay there until I got my first check, and then I could rent one of the rooms in her house. There were no 'until' terms that would signal the end of our agreement, so I accepted without hesitation. Especially being that the next morning I would have to vacate the motel room anyway. With a quick trip to the motel and back, she showed me her modest little house. My room was actually the living room on the couch, which spurred a quick reminder of Rudy's couch and gave me a chill down my spine.

The situation worked out fairly well for about a month. I switched to the third shift which saw me arriving at the house as her daughter was leaving for school. I would give her a ride to school and return to sleep, while Linda would spend her usual day at the bar drinking. When she would get home, it would be about time for me to go pickup her daughter while Linda prepared our modest dinner. Time after dinner was mostly watching her television shows over-the-air, since she couldn't afford cable. The choice was cable TV or the bar all day, and she made her best choice.

That situation came to an abrupt halt, again. While I was sleeping during the day after taking a few extra hours at the factory, Linda came to the house early and woke me up. She told me to get off the couch and get ready. As tired as I was, I assumed that I had overslept and needed to leave and fetch her daughter from school. As I grabbed my keys, she stopped me to ask where I was going. That's when I noticed the time and that it was barely noon. She was asking for help in cleaning the house.

As strange as it sounds, she never once told me that she had a son. He was on his way from Florida, and would be arriving tonight. She filled me in, but it all sounded really vague to me. He had been in and youth facility and just turned eighteen, so they released him. I had heard in conversations she had with others, that her ex-husband had left money to the kids for when they turned eighteen, but there was never mention of the son at all.

He had apparently been released earlier in the week, the lawyer gave him a portion of the money, and he bought a car and pointed it this way. My emotions were all over the place. She was excited to see her son again, which I could feel and thought was wonderful. But on the other hand, he was just getting out of a "youth facility" aka kiddie prison and coming this way.

I was assured again, there would be no issues and I would be fine with our current arrangements. This was of course not the case. Within two days of her son's arrival, I was informed quietly by her son, that I was not welcome there and had to leave. It was strange, but at the same time understandable. What frustrated me the most was that they still expected some sort of payment after I left, and still expected to come chauffeur the daughter to school after work. Yeah, that's not happening.

That arrangement had to end in any case, as the schedule was changing too much. In my usual sleep time, he was there and had friends with him. Mostly lounging on the couch drinking beer and smoking pot. That makes it really difficult to survive the ten hour shift through the night.

The Salvation Army Hotel, sort of

It took a little bit of convincing, but I found a room in the downtown area. The Salvation Army in that town had three rooms upstairs from their office and store areas. They would rent them to single desperate men for slightly less than the motel charged for the week. There was a shared bathroom and no kitchen facilities. The rules were simple, except for the hours. No women were allowed at all, which was no issue for me. But the entry and exit hours were set in stone, as they did not want issues with neighbors or maybe they just needed to feel in control. I had to leave extremely early for work, and wait in my truck an hour for the door to open before I could return to my room. Minor inconvenience, but I made it work for about a month.

During one of my regular check-in calls, I was requested to come back for a hearing on the case. So I made the drive in my old Mazda pickup truck, back into the gang's territory.

This time, I was able to stay at my grandmother's house and sleep in her spare bedroom. For a few hours I considered staying and just hiding in plain site, living in her spare room. But my job expected me back in two days and I was getting close to being offered a permanent position. I had made an impression apparently and they liked me. I wasn't really sure if I could handle the daily death of a thousand cuts, but it was permanent work with benefits.

I stayed at my grandmother's house awaiting a call from the State's Attorney's office for all of Monday. Late morning on Tuesday, I called them for a time to be at the courthouse. The receptionist informed me that the hearing was cancelled early Monday afternoon and I wasn't going to be needed for at least a month. I would think that a phone call as we arranged would be nice in this situation, but maybe there was too much to keep track of. I just left it at that, without much anger other than the cost of my travel.

I started my drive back a day early, planning to just take a day to myself and take a different route avoiding the interstate. My parents and other family members had always taken that route, but I never had. I always took the interstate for as much of the trip as I could. But this time, it was nearly summer and I had the time.

When I returned back, everything started to fall back into the same pace. Nothing had really changed other than the weather. I had arrived in the winter, but summer was starting to creep in. My room was starting to get hot during the day, and you can be sure that a charity is not going to spend money on air conditioning. That room got so hot that my large box fan could not move enough air to get you anywhere close to comfortable. There was no way I would be able to sleep during the daytime in that heat.

After about a week of dealing with this, my mother came into town. She was on her way to Tennessee for a get together similar to a high school reunion, but not official. She asked if I wanted to go with her for the weekend. Being that I hardly ever got to spend time with her, I made the effort and requested another weekend off. I would find on my return that it was in fact not alright, and that I did lose my job over this trip.

We spent that weekend in Cookeville Tennessee visiting with a few friends from her high school days, as well as a couple distance relatives that also lived in the area. I became fast friends with the sons of one of her friends, which is where I spent my portion of that weekend. I was extended a welcome in the case I found myself in the area and needed a place to stay. I felt like part of their family, even though I had only spent a few days with them.

A touch of farming – but I wrecked it

It didn't take me long to find another job, mostly due to it being such a heavy agricultural area. I was able to find a job on my own with the local farm co-op. The co-op provided farm products to all the corn and bean farmers in the area as well as services that some of the smaller farmers cannot afford themselves. They had large fertilizer and spraying equipment, as well as large bins, silos, and other vehicles and buildings.

My job was to prepare mixed fertilizers in bulk for the large spreading equipment. Also to fill, deliver, and pick up anhydrous tanks (anhydrous ammonia) that farmers used when preparing or maintaining their fields. These were purpose built two-axle trailers that were nothing more than a steel frame holding up a huge white pill-shaped tank. If you've spent any time in a mid-western farming area while in season, you've surely seen them.

I was able to get my agricultural commercial driver's license, as a seasonal agricultural worker, allowing me to pull the tank trailers. This is where I spent most of my summer, until I was found by the gang.

I had been delivering anhydrous tanks through the day, but was asked to pick up empty trailers on my way back. I was inexperienced at how these loads should be hauled and almost took my own life at the cost of not knowing. The farmer had used only one of his tanks and left a full one to be returned as well, but left them side by side in the field. I was in a rush since it was late already and we never got paid overtime, so I  connected the trailers to the truck as fast as I could. My mistake was not checking the levels to find out that one was still full. I had the full tank at the rear, with the light empty trailer in the middle.

Getting out of the field and on the road was easy enough, but the fifty mile per hour curve ahead almost claimed my life. I had let off the pedal as I approached the long sweeping curve. Expecting to need to accelerate on the way out, the tug at the rear of the truck caught me by surprise. Followed by my own trailer being within reach had I put my arm out the window. The heavier full trailer was acting like a whip and pulled the truck into a spin as it gained momentum. The truck was slowing quickly as it spun around before grabbing traction as the trailer broke free from the hitch. I recall briefly seeing one trailer rolling sideways down the road and the other bouncing end over end into a freshly planted corn field. That's when the pole jumped out in front of the truck.

This is the first experience I had with an airbag, and it must have done a great job. I had to have been going at least forty miles per hour as I hit the pole head on. I found later that there were actually three poles there, as the utility company had replaced it a few times due to previous accidents, but never pulled out the previously broken ones. We know now that it takes three poles to stop a full size Dodge diesel pickup truck, there wasn't more than a fresh chip in the wood. But the truck was totaled.

The co-op had two-way radios in all of their equipment, so it wasn't long before help arrived. Everybody at the co-op came out to the site to help handle the situation. My boss, who managed the co-op, took me to the hospital to get checked out. I wasn't fired, but had to take a few days off at the doctor's advice. It was when I returned that I figured it out.

I took a drive out to the co-op office on the evening before my return to work the next day and was pulled into the office for a chat. I figured I was about to finally get fired over the accident, but was mistaken. I was instead reprimanded for having friends show up and refuse to leave for hours on end. The day after the accident, there were two guys that showed up, dressed in "city clothes" as my boss called them. As we talked, I was gaining more information which led to being told that these "two Mexican guys driving an older blue Oldsmobile with gold trim, and Illinois license plates", and that they both spoke to each other. This was very uncommon in this area. There was no doubt in my mind, they somehow had found me.

Straight Outta Indiana -- and into Tennessee

I had seen that car parked in the lot across the street from the room I was living in. It had been there both days I had stayed in my room and when I walked to the store for food. They were parked next to my truck both times I spotted the car, but it didn't register with me until that moment. The next day, I didn't go to work.

I grabbed my backpack and whatever else I could fit into a gym bag and slipped out the back door. Outside of filling in a few people that I was leaving town, I didn't make any stops. I sat down the street from the parking lot, watching that car and my truck, waiting for the opportunity to leave. But it didn't take long, and I could see them slowly back from their parking spot and drive down to the gas station at the end of the block. I took my chance, slipped into my truck and took the back way out of town.

First heading to the east to another nearby town, before making a turn to the south. Following a paper map, I found my way the long way around back to Cookeville Tennessee. I arrived late during the night, and thought it best to sleep in my truck. I had only been here for a weekend, over a month before, but I could remember my way around town. Parking in a dark parking lot for the night, that morning I returned where I was previously extended a welcome.

We sat in the yard talking for hours, and I'm sure there were phone calls to my mother to verify what was being said. But after that long explanation and some parenting by these fine folks, I was offered a place to stay, again. Another couch in an unused living room. They used their family room mostly as it had easy access to the backyard and driveway. They spent most of the daylight hours outside in the yard anyway.

Most of this I have forgotten, but what I do remember is quite vivid. The husband loved to toss horseshoes behind the garage, and they spent every evening sitting by a fire pit in the backyard. Any time I try sitting around a fire at night, this whole situation fills my head, and is the reason I cannot enjoy evenings sitting around a campfire.

They were some of the happiest people I had met in my life. I never heard even the slightest disagreement or raised voice. They had two sons, one was slightly older than me, and one younger, but I do not remember the younger of the two at all. The oldest had shaved his head during his senior year in high school, and it still wouldn't grow back. With my already receding hairline and his premature baldness, we could completely relate to each other.

I spent the early summer working as a go-fer (aka "go-fer that tool, go-fer that pipe") for a decent size plumbing company. My only memory of that experience was my boss mistaking an abandoned septic tank for an abandoned well, and sending me in to "find the pump at the bottom". They don't really stink when everything is dried up, but after you break the surface it's another story. I had a few rounds of injections over that one.

I wasn't making enough money at that job to go anywhere. I wasn't an apprentice or training for anything, just a go-fer. I was assigned to one of the old guys who was sent on random jobs for the owner. He didn't really have a position there, but was doing it to pass the time after retirement. The owner had some connection with him that I never knew the details of, but it was enough that he held a job and was assigned me as a helper.

I made my regular check-in call to the police captain that I was 'assigned'. Letting him know where I was, that everything was still ok, and to ask about future appearances. I had already spoken to him when I arrived, and gave him my contact information. I had even checked in early once, only because I was anxious to get this all behind me. But they were never in a hurry and I felt they dragged it out for whatever reasons. But I was really getting attached to the area and the people. I could see myself staying down there and never returning to Illinois. I just had to figure out a better work situation if I was ever to get out on my own. My welcome never seemed to wear out and I made myself as useful as I possibly could, offering to help with anything they were needing.

This check-in call was different. The captain seemed frustrated with my call, almost as if I was asking him for something that I did not deserve or nagging him way too often. It was my regular time frame to call and I asked if the schedule changed or if there was a return date for me yet. I could hear him grind his teeth slightly, as if it was the sound of my voice. That's when he told me that I need to get up there by Monday morning. The excitement choked me up and it took me a few seconds to reply, but I told him I would be on the next bus. He hung up on me, but I didn't care and didn't read anything into it. I was looking forward to everything being behind me.

I miss those people and the way I felt when I was treated like family. Unfortunately, I never returned to Cookeville Tennessee ever again.

Arrested – "for my own protection"

I arrived fairly early in the morning on a greyhound. My mother had said that she would be waiting to take me to my grandmother's house and I would call the captain as soon as I arrived.

The greyhound station in town had closed years before, and all busses instead stopped at a gas station just off the interstate. They were a ticket agent as well as a purveyor of cigarettes, beer, and gas. But the lot was large enough for the bus and open enough that you could see every vehicle parked and waiting. I never saw my mother's car, and I figure that it wasn't there anyway. But I did notice the black unmarked police cruiser. No sooner than the bus stopped, two detectives climbed aboard and walked directly to me, calling me by name.

I was escorted off the bus and handcuffed the moment my feet hit the pavement. Nobody else got off the bus until I was placed into the squad car and the detectives threw a thumbs up to the driver and waved to somebody inside the gas station. I was taken directly to the county jail without any explanation from the detectives. I did not recognize either of them, but knew they were completely legit from the car, clothes, and the way they spoke. They made idle chat between themselves, but refused to speak a word to me.

The State's Attorney charged me with 'Criminal Drug Conspiracy', citing cocaine they claimed to have found in the motel room, a class X felony. This is the highest class of felony within the state of Illinois outside of capital murder. But, they only charged me. There was no grand jury, no pre-trial, nothing. I was never arrested at the time, never fingerprinted, and immediately released after the talks with the State's Attorney.

This time, they arrested me. They had already arrested all the gang members that I remembered, except for one.

The shooter, Roman Medel Jr, had escaped the area before he could be arrested. He eventually turned up after these events in Mexico, but the county decided not to pursue the agreed extradition from Mexico and bring him back after the FBI made the arrangements.

At my bond hearing, the state's attorney that I had been involved with requested a bond of ten-thousand dollars, which I could not obtain. Illinois is a cash bond state, meaning that I only had to produce ten percent, or one-thousand dollars. But that one-thousand dollars might as well have been ten-million, I couldn't get it. I was being used to pressure the defendants, dangled in front of them like bait. I was placed into protective custody within the jail, but paraded in front of them at any given opportunity. I can recall trips to the courthouse for no other purpose than to be placed in a holding cell right beside them.

A few days later my bond was paid, by somebody I did not recognize. I was not released that night, but instead taken to the courthouse the next morning where my bond was increased to a hundred thousand dollars, to keep me from leaving. Amazingly, that bond was paid too. I still had no clue what was happening. Again, not released. Another trip to the courthouse where the state's attorney wanted to talk to me finally, after again changing my bond amount. His star witness, "Bo" was refusing to talk, so he finally decided to have a conversation with me. This time my bond was changed simply to 'NO BOND', I wasn't going anywhere.

He asked about the source of my previous bond funds, but I had no clue where it was coming from. There is a name attached obviously, but I don't recognize it. And they can't associate the name with anyone they have in the system. It appears to be some random person bailing me out of jail. I was the only inmate within the jail not charged with murder or escape, that has 'no bail'. The courthouse gossip got back to the jail as usual, and the tales started spinning. I became a jail rock star, nothing to be proud of by any means, but it got the petty thugs in my pod off my back. Probably out of fear of something they didn't know about me.

Another few trips to the courthouse, and again my name isn't on the docket for anything. I didn't have any hearing dates scheduled and I hadn't even met the attorney the judge assigned to me. I figure it's another one of those days. Sure enough, parade after parade, blatantly showing me to the guys that I'm there to testify against.

Then came the day of a pre-trial hearing typically within weeks of their actual trial due to start. I was placed alone across the courtroom from them in the jury box, looking directly at the group of them on the other side of the room. Even the judge recognized the maneuver and made a comment that I could not hear, but understood it was aimed towards me. A few hand gestures from the defendants came my way, the usual finger across the throat, but thankfully I had no emotion left and was incapable of showing fear or anything else. Eventually the bait on the hook stops wiggling, and this is me, bait on a hook. Within a few minutes I got ushered back down into the holding cells and eventually transported back to the main jail, on the same bus with them.

When I get back to the jail, one of the guards tells me that he heard a rumor that all of them took a plea deal. I would finally be getting out of jail. I was released later in the week after their plea's became official and all of them accepted their agreed sentences.

The people that you meet in jail

I was finally set to be released after several months being dangled as bait in front of gang members that tried to kill me.

During my time in protective custody, I was housed within a pod that was reserved for witnesses(snitches) and old guys. In jail, the safety of inmates awaiting trial is supposed to be important, so they get their own pod. Since a jail has a finite capacity, these areas need to be shared for other purposes. Some pods are separated by dividers and this one was no different. One quarter of this pod was administrative segregation. Movie fans will recognize this as 'the hole' or solitary confinement. The remainder of the space housed the elderly inmates as well as those also being held as witnesses.

This is where I met Dave. There were a few older guys that I came to know over my months spent in D pod. They were friendly, but still accused criminals awaiting trial. But they were good for a card game to pass the time. You can only watch so many soap operas with the guards.

We weren't on lockdown nearly as much as the other pods within the jail. The inmates here just weren't much trouble. Most needed a cane to get from one area to another, and it typically took them a while to get back into their cells. The guards actually considered this posting as a reward, mostly due to not having to do anything. They had their places just in front of, and below the guard desk countertop, where they could sit at one of our tables and play cards with us. Of course we gambled, but nothing they wanted since they could acquire coffee, tea bags, and commissary candy bars much better than what we had to offer. They enjoyed the break from the boredom when they couldn't nap.

I met Dave within a week of getting placed in D pod. We always seemed to end up at the same table. In the other pods within the jail, the game was always spades or hearts. But I was learning to play Pinochle and some other games that I remember my grandmother playing. Pinochle and Euchre were the primary games here, and somehow I always ended up with Dave as a partner.

We talked a lot outside the card games and I felt that I got to know him well. He knew my story and heard all of the rumors going around the jail regarding the gang member trials I was a witness and victim of. I never got the whole story for what he was being charged with, and it honestly never occurred to me to ask. I wasn't proud of being in jail, but I wasn't hiding it either, since it was already known far and wide. But his charges, I was never aware of.

I always felt comfortable talking to him and he seemed to give good counsel, and at least I felt better finally talking to someone. I would not recognize until much later, some of the signs. Being inexperienced socially, there were signs that should have given me a warning. But I was thinking only of myself at that time in life, so I never stopped talking.

We talked and played cards for months, he talked me down from panic attacks after being paraded and dangled in front of my attackers at the courthouse. This whole time he was absorbing everything I said and processing a plan. It had previously been attempted to bond me out by an unknown person. This was an obvious attempt to either bribe me or finish what they started, so I would not testify against them. No victim/witness, no conviction.

Dave had done his research and decided that once I got released, that the applied bond which was still on my books, would become available to me. Sure enough, the bail rules show that any bond applied in the way it was submitted became security applied to my account. After which time my case was disposed of, I should be given that money by the court. Since Illinois is a cash bond state, the responsibility of another person is only applied for bonds documents or real estate securities. I am not sure if this has changed over the years, but it applied at this time.

Dave had a plan, that since it wasn't really MY money, but I would gain access to it, I could have it applied to his bond. In exchange, he would arrange for a safe place for me to live after release, along with one thousand dollars which his girlfriend at the time would give me in exchange until the bond transferred and Dave was released. I did not believe any of it, and chalked it up as jailhouse bullshit.

Until I got a request for a visit from a lady named Pearl. Pearl was Dave's girlfriend. Since the request came during one of the very limited times we were on lockdown, I couldn't talk to Dave about it. So I took the visit. The visitation area is upstairs and within view of most of the cells in the pod. Dave's cell was well within view of the visitation area, so I was sure that he was aware.

When Pearl arrived behind the thick glass, I saw an older woman that would give you the 'somebody's grandmother' feeling. I picked up the phone and listened as she spoke. She told me how Dave has changed for the better emotionally and she thanked me for spending time with him. She had been worried about his health and mental well-being, up until I befriended him. Since then he sounded stable and less depressed than he had been leading up to the point we met. She also told me how excited that he was about the possibility of being able to get out of jail during his trial by my bail assignment.

I lost it. I was only thinking of myself. I never had agreed to it, but there it was staring me in the face. I was going to use that money to make another attempt at starting again, at least a thousand miles from here. That guy dropped off cash on my account, he's got to know that he's not getting it back. Although I suspect it belongs to a gang member.

But looking through the glass at Pearl, she was excited too. You could see the appreciation and hope that they would spend time together. She told me that I would be staying in her spare bedroom in her house, gave me the address and phone number, and told me of the meals she would cook. How could I say no? It wasn't my money anyway. I agreed.

Later in the day I finally spoke to Dave. He told me that she had not told him that she was coming, and that it's not her typical day to visit. He seemed saddened that he didn't get to see or speak to her. Until I told him that I agreed with his plan.

Somehow I knew you would keep me

The day of my release was interesting to say the least. I was ordered released by the judge at the courthouse in the early afternoon. Upon returning to the jail, I was put back into the pod with everyone else. A few knew that I was getting out that day and congratulated me, probably for surviving so long. But you could see Dave's eyes light up and a grin from ear to ear when he heard the news. But, hours passed and not a single call at the guard desk.

I asked a few times and was told to sit down and shut up. After more back and forth I got into it verbally with one of the guards. I didn't care about lockdown since I was due to be released any time now. But I had a rude awakening during that lockdown. They weren't releasing me.

There was another state that I had an unresolved issue, a small mess that I had to clean up, and these guys weren't playing. They probably spoke to the State's Attorney here and were convinced by him to come and get me. They were sending an officer to come pick me up. The next morning after breakfast, sure enough the door popped open. I was hoping to hear the news of my release. But instead I was handed directly over to a police officer from another state. We drove for a while to get back to his jail. I spent over a week there.

I had attempted on occasion to contact Pearl to pass on the word that I could be tied up with this. My bail was two-hundred dollar's cash, but I didn't have a dime. I found out later that Pearl had taken a small vacation with her family and had been out of town for a week. As soon as she got into the house and heard the message I left her, she sat by her phone waiting for my call.

After slightly over a week, I decided to call again and she answered immediately. I was happy to hear another person's voice since the section of the jail I was in was nearly empty. One of the dirty jails you see on television that has been forgotten by time and hasn't been cleaned in a decade.

She told me that she would arrange bail and we would figure things out from there. I fully expected her to call the jail with a credit card or something, but she had other plans.

Later that night I heard my name called, so I walked up to an open cellblock door. Pearl had made the drive, cash in hand and bailed me out. After processing, I was told that my grandmother from Illinois was down the street at the diner waiting. When I got to her, it was a quiet and brief hug and she handed me her car keys. The drive had wiped this poor woman out, she was exhausted. I was energized, especially having been so rested from the time spent doing nothing in a jail cell. I made the trip with only a single stop for the restroom and fuel while she slept in the backseat. When we arrived at her house, she pointed me to the spare bedroom and she retired to her room.

The next morning, I lived up to my agreement and called the court clerk. There was a hold on the bail money and was told that it could take thirty to sixty days for the release of bail funds. It didn't matter what I said to the clerk's office, they weren't letting go of those funds. I relayed the news to Pearl who relayed to Dave. Even though it seemed like an eternity to them, they were still happy with the plan and I was invited to stay for the duration.

A home, a car, a family? – just a dream

During my stay at Pearl's house, I was treated as a welcomed guest. I had a place to sleep, access to food, and Pearl offered the use of her vehicle whenever I needed to go someplace. I did not travel too often, as I still feared being found by the gang. Thankfully they never really travelled to this far side of town… those were the days.

Pearl decided that I should have a car of my own. I had started doing side jobs and also held a job telemarketing, so I had an income. For the second time in my life, I was asked what kind of car I preferred and my answer never changed. I wanted a Mustang convertible, that much never changed.

Pearl had a job, and went to work daily. I do not recall what she did, but I think it was secretarial. One day on her way home from work, she spotted a silver mustang GT at a local car dealer on the front line. She took it upon herself to stop and talk to a salesman about it. When she arrived home later than her usual, of course I asked about the delay. I was worried that she had car troubles or something else. That's when she told me to get in her car and we were going somewhere.

Pearl drove us right up to the front door of the dealer, where this 1990 Mustang GT convertible was parked. She had bought the car, with an extended warranty and handed me the keys. I am fresh out of jail, twenty-two years old, and finally feeling like the 'spoiled' kid I had been accused of being all of my life, and it was basically a stranger doing the spoiling. But then came the kicker of the payments. She was taken advantage of by the dealer, and even I knew it. The price, the rate, the payment, were all well outside anything I had ever seen before. I had worked for the sleaziest Pontiac dealer in the state, so I could see through the deal the moment I glanced at the paperwork. But worse was the payment. No matter how you slice it, I couldn't afford it. I couldn't afford anything really. Pearl assured me "it will be ok, go enjoy yourself" as she handed me the paperwork including an insurance card with my name added to her policy. Did I really have that much of an effect on her life that I deserved this? Never, something was fishy.

At this point in time, I had met a girl. During this point, the internet was something totally new and completely obscure to most people. But I had an affinity towards it. I knew it was the next big thing that would change our culture, so I feared nothing. The girl I met actually lived in Massachusetts, that I met in a chat room on America Online. This was when free trial diskettes and CDs were commonplace on store checkout counters. Repeated new accounts meant almost unlimited free access, which I repeatedly took advantage of.

We spoke nightly on the telephone, using the telemarketing company's dime. I couldn't afford those lengthy calls, but they had me calling all over the country anyway. No, they never said a word as I was able to sell burn cream to the devil.

After weeks of endless night long calls, she had enough of her life in Massachusetts and decided that she wanted to take the next step and move to Illinois with me. I had told her about my arrangements with Pearl, but not with Dave. She knew that I was living there and helping out, and without a stable job. But she felt that she needed to get away from her troubles there.

One night her phone did not ring when I called. Instead I got the tones and automated voice in my ear telling me that her number was no longer in service. I thought that it was over and she decided to move on, or she simply couldn't cover her phone bill after the few times she had called me directly. That is, until my phone rang at 5am the next morning.

She had fallen asleep at the wheel of her car that was jam packed with all the belongings that she could fit inside. The car was off the side of the interstate in Ohio and she was calling me from a rest area on the toll road. Her car was being towed out and she was losing her mind. After a few minutes I had calmed her down and told her I would be on my way.

Pearl was up and about the house at this time, getting ready for work, I filled her in on the situation. For a moment, you could see the shock on her face, that this girl just hopped in her car. But mostly it was because she barely knew what was going on, as all of our conversations were late at night when Pearl had gone to bed.

I never spoke much about the girl to Pearl, as she had enough on her mind. But her shock switched to an immediate smile. Pearl was an awesome woman. She understood the situation and that it was too late to change anything, and she invited her to stay at the house as well.

I pointed the Mustang east and put the pedal down. Two speeding tickets on the toll road shouldn't be too terrible--they bit me in the ass later in life. I finally locate her sitting on a bench in the rest area munching on French fries. Our first face to face meeting, and she's sitting in a rest area shoving French fries into her mouth as if she's never eaten a fried potato in her whole life… how romantic.

We leave to locate her car at the tow yard and they allow her to grab some things from it. I would be back in a few days to get the car and we estimated the bill depending on the day I picked it up. I was told that the car was not drivable, but it rolls fine. Later I would borrow a moving van and car dolly to go get it and tow it back to Illinois.

Other than the crappy job and weird living arrangements, I'm starting to feel like I have a new life. As well as a new "Aunt Pearl" as we both started to call her. I won't bother with giving you the girl's name, since she didn't stick around for very long.

We knew this wouldn't last

It was about a week of peaceful living and we all got along good in the house. She was looking for a job as I repaired her car. It took me less than a day to repair the girl's car and make it roadworthy again. It still had scuffs and scratches from its trip off the side of the road, but it ran and drove as a car should.

This when I finally found some paperwork regarding Dave's arrest. I was never the nosey type, so I never bothered to question anything. I assumed he was a thief or something like that. But no, it was HUGE. I was completely floored. Me and the girl immediately packed the cars and left.

Dave was heading to trial for sexual abuse of a child. Pearl had been actively hiding it from me, but she left out a single bit of paperwork from Dave's lawyer and I found it on the kitchen counter. The incident occurred with her own grandson, yet she still sided with Dave.

That was the last I ever saw of Pearl, but I spoke to her once after. I never heard of Dave again. I turned my back and ran. That same day I located an apartment in a town thirty miles north and sold both of my computers to pay for it.

Earlier the same day that we discovered the Dave information, was the day we had gotten married. There was no planning or thinking behind it. We decided that we both wanted to be married, why not to each other? We were both standing there, so it happened. We were both young and naive. I did meet with my mother earlier and let her know of the plans beforehand, as well as invite her to the courthouse. But she chose not to attend, and I wasn't really surprised.

So here I am, married to a girl I hardly know. Living in an apartment that I definitely cannot afford, and driving a car that is in Pearl's name that I am responsible for the payments. I did contact Pearl via leaving her a message and delivering the car to her driveway to deal with. But magically a day later, it showed back up in the apartment parking lot and the keys under the windshield wiper with a note telling me to keep it and just make the payments, that she understands.

I eventually got into contact with the court clerk to make sure they didn't apply the bail money to Dave. But I learned that the bond money was already refunded to an attorney representing the person that held the matching receipt. I honestly wasn't even mad. Even with my feeling that it was an attempt to take my life to prevent me from testifying, that took some level of bravery in getting that money back. It was just as obvious to the state's attorney, but there would be no evidence to link a suspicion to it creating a crime. Oh well, I was dealing with 'today issues' and not dreams and fairy tales.

I had lost my job at the telemarketing company over the commute. I just couldn't make it work for the pay. I immediately got a job at the local Target as an early morning shelf stocker, which was the only position I could find. Luckily it was even within walking distance in the snow.

She got a job as a printing press operator with a longer commute than I had already lost a job over. For a little over a month, we made it work. But not long after, she had decided that this was too much for her and she left. She headed back to Massachusetts in the middle of the night, while I was working an extra shift. I came in the midnight before to move shelves and clean, before my morning stock shift.

I came home that morning to a nearly empty apartment, aside from the crappy furniture you would expect for some seriously poor people trying to make it work. I still had a junk computer that the second hand store wouldn't touch. But it got me back on America Online, so I spent my evenings crying into the keyboard, and by day I stocked shelves or slept.

I still could not afford to pay for the car, so that was also the topic of some of my chat room drama. I had managed to find people that shared similar events in their lives, so it helped to share the latest happenings along with everyone else. Eventually, I watched as the repo guy came for the car. I wasn't heartbroken other than losing a really cool car for that time in my life. I already walked to work and passed a grocery store on the way. I didn't really need a car.

Ending a miserable year positively

I was less than a week and I was already spending way too much time in the chat rooms. I was avoiding life altogether, except one neighbor who I worked with. He was going to trade school during the day and worked at Target for extra money. But I started riding to work with him and walked home since he drove from there to school.

In one of my random chat rooms that I frequented, I started to get familiar with a few people. We all had similar strange relationship issues and got along really well. I started talking regularly to another girl from the east coast and apparently hadn't learned my lesson. But there must be something about those east coast girls that make them irresistible. I started spending more and more time chatting privately instead of the main chatroom, which turned into phone calls. I knew that I couldn't afford the calls, but honestly had no intention of paying the bill anyway. I knew my time was coming to an end and something drastic was due to happen. Surely an unpaid phone bill wasn't going to make a difference, but I needed that contact with another person.

We hit it off really well, and she knew everything about me already. I was an open book. Sure I lied about a few things, I was a 20-something guy talking to a girl, we all lied to hide rough edges. And boy were my edges rough.

The day I received a five-day warning for eviction was when I lost it completely. I immediately fell into the chat rooms and started pouring my heart out. I was totally lost and had no clue where to turn. I wasn't out cruising for a relationship, I was looking for someone to talk to, and hopefully some useful advice. There had to be someone that had some knowledge or experience that I didn't have.

I never had anyone I could talk to the way I could with her. We talked through the night and past the time I would normally go to work. I could care less about work, what's the point? I had just been paid and when the previous girl left, she took every dime. I wouldn't be able to make up for the rent with the next paycheck and it was nowhere near the amount I needed. The rent would take two people, and that isn't happening. In the eyes of any employer, I was an uneducated criminal drug dealer with zero experience at anything.

At approximately 4am, nearing the end of our conversation, she asked me a question that totally changed my life. "If I sent you a plane ticket? Would you get on the plane?"

I packed one small box and a backpack. I walked away from everything I've known, with no fear and only hope. My neighbor was off work for the week and heading home for the rest of the holiday, so he gave me a ride to the airport. I was about to meet my future wife for the first time, and spend New Year's Eve 1995 with her in upstate New York. I feel that she saved my life, and we are still happily married to this day.

About the Author

Let me be clear, I am a nobody.

I am not a public figure. I have not made any notable contributions to our society. I have been arrested and in jail. I have sold and consumed drugs. I have stolen out of desire as well as need. I have been a bad person. I try to be a good person. I have had office jobs, worked construction, farmed, drove truck, and many more undesirable jobs. I have campaigned for and advised small town politicians. I have been married, divorced, and married again. I have no children, but have provided for two children for a few years when I was younger. I have been healthy and unhealthy.

I am a nobody. But here I am, finally grown up.